Brain Gym

LEVEL 4

Written by: Laura Miller
Series Editor: Melanie Williams

Pearson Education Limited
Edinburgh Gate, Harlow,
Essex CM20 2JE, England
and Associated Companies throughout the world.

ISBN: 978-1-4082-8815-3

This edition first published by Pearson Education Ltd 2013
11
Text copyright © Pearson Education Ltd 2013

The moral rights of the author have been asserted
in accordance with the Copyright Designs and Patents Act 1988

Set in 17/21pt OT Fiendstar
Printed in China
SWTC/11

Acknowledgements
The publisher would like to thank the following for their kind permission to reproduce their photographs:
(Key: b-bottom; c-centre; l-left; r-right; t-top)

Alamy Images: allOver photography 6tl, 22t, Mark Bassett 3 (mobile), Danita Delimont 4cr, rgbstudio 6bl, RubberBall 6br; **Corbis:** MedicalRF.com 5t; **DK Images:** Angela Coppola 11br; **Fotolia.com:** Alexander Yakovlev 11tr, Adrian Costea 3 (bottle), e-python 15 (mug), Eisenhans 6bc, grandeduc 3 (headphones), lesart777 15 (toy boat), m.u.ozmen 16 (chocolate), 17 (chocolate), mates 16-17 (tea), picsfive 15 (pencil), plotnik 4c, Popova Olga 21 (socks), Silkstock 3 (pencil), voisine 20tl; **Getty Images:** UpperCut Images 11tl, Katrina Wittkamp 10l; **PhotoDisc:** Photolink 3 (football); **Science Photo Library Ltd:** Simon Fraser 5b; **Shutterstock.com:** 3445128471 6tr, aarrows 14 (cheese), Anna Kucherova 16 (banana), Anneka 17 (child blindfolded), Artur Synenko 15 (hair brush), AVAVA 20tr, boumen&japet 21 (shoes), Dionisvera 4l, donatas1205 14 (milk), DUSAN ZIDAR 16 (fish), Eternalfeelings 15 (eraser), Evgeny Karandaev 15 (flower), Fotocrisis 14 (icecream), FoxPictures 3 (laptop), Gregory Gerber 16 (cheese), Darrin Henry 5c, higyou 3 (bath), Julia Ivantsova 16 (spoon), 17 (teaspoon), Kletr 3 (bicycle), Igor Klimov 14 (egg), Komar Maria 14 (chicken), Lev Kropotov 7c, 10r, Lucie Lang 14 (banana), markrhiggins 15 (glasses), Maxx-Studio 15 (phone), mikeledray 3 (brain), 4br, Morgan Lane Photography 7b, Nattika 16 (orange), Orla 6c (face outline), Pixelbliss 14 (bread), Renewer 16 (scarf), Ruth Black 14 (cakes), Sashkin 15 (ball), Sergey Andrianov 16 (apple), sextoacto 9, Alex Staroseltsev 14 (chocolate), TerraceStudio 15 (hat), Tischenko Irina 15 (butterfly), Tobik 16-17 (butter), Ulises Sepúlveda Déniz 7tl, wheatley 15 (coins), Xpixel 11bl, YAKOBCHUK VASYL 6c (brain), 24, Yuri Arcurs 21 (boy), 21 (girl), 22c, 22cl; **SuperStock:** Design Pics 6tc; University of Wisconsin and Michigan State Comparative Mammalian Brain Collections, the National Museum of Health and Medicine. The preparation of images has been funded by the **National Science Foundation**, as well as by the **National Institutes of Health: 7 (monkey's brain), 7tr, 7cr**
Cover images: Front: **Shutterstock.com:** sextoacto

All other images © Pearson Education

In some instances we have been unable to trace the owners of copyright material,
and we would appreciate any information that would enable us to do so.

Illustrations: Clare Elsom

For a complete list of the titles available in the Pearson English Kids Readers series, please go to
www.pearsonenglishkidsreaders.com. Alternatively, write to your local Pearson Education office or to
Pearson English Readers Marketing Department, Pearson Education, Edinburgh Gate, Harlow, Essex CM20 2JE, England.

Do you use any of these things every day? Which thing do you use the most? Are you pointing at the brain? You use your brain all the time.

It is like a very intelligent computer inside your head.

brain

You can eat, sleep, run, jump and think, all because of your brain!

Your brain is inside your head. But what does your brain look like?

Like this?

Or like this?

Or perhaps like this?

It looks like all three! It looks a bit funny but is the most important part of your body. A person cannot live without a brain.

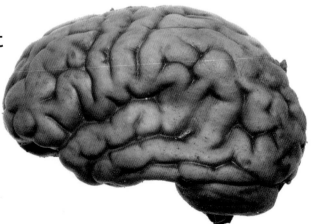

Your brain has got two halves.

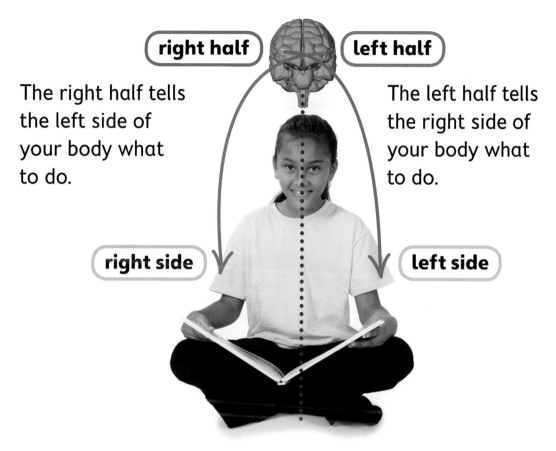

right half

left half

The right half tells the left side of your body what to do.

The left half tells the right side of your body what to do.

right side

left side

This is a busy brain. It gets messages from different parts of the body and sends messages at the same time.

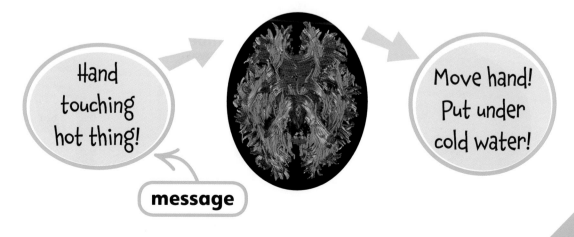

Hand touching hot thing!

Move hand! Put under cold water!

message

Different parts of your brain help you do different things, like balancing, remembering or talking. Here is a different picture of your brain. It shows the different parts of your brain and what they do. All the parts work together.

seeing

smelling and tasting

balancing

moving

remembering

listening

talking

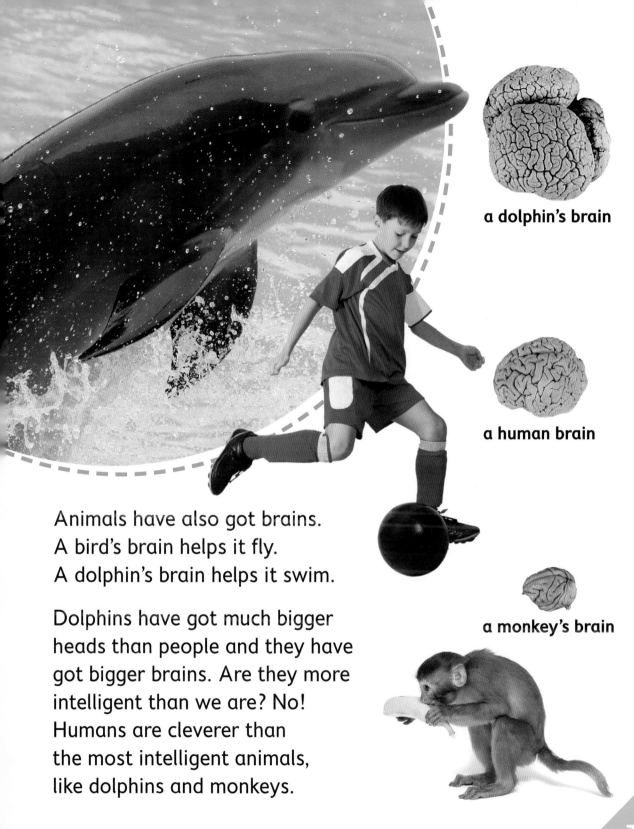

a dolphin's brain

a human brain

a monkey's brain

Animals have also got brains.
A bird's brain helps it fly.
A dolphin's brain helps it swim.

Dolphins have got much bigger heads than people and they have got bigger brains. Are they more intelligent than we are? No! Humans are cleverer than the most intelligent animals, like dolphins and monkeys.

The size of humans' brains is not important. People with larger heads are no more intelligent than people with smaller heads. But it is important to exercise your brain. It cannot get bigger, but it can work better!

Come on!
Let's do some exercises for your brain.

Can you read this?

What about this?

Turn the book round. Now you can read it! it is easy!

And this one?

What coms aftr "d" and bfor "f"?

a, b, c, d, ?, f ...

Are you ready for more?
Read on!

Sometimes keeping still can exercise your brain. But it is not always easy. Can you do these balancing exercises?

① Tree

Put your right foot high on the inside of your left leg.

Put your arms up.

Look up.

Close your eyes!

Closing your eyes makes your brain work harder.

② Dancer

Hold your right foot behind you in your right hand.

Pull your foot up behind you.

Put your left arm up.

Close your eyes!

③ Bird

Put your hands on the ground.

Put your knees high on your arms.

Bring your face down and lift your toes.

Moving in new ways can be difficult, but it is also good exercise for your brain.

1 Up, down and round

Rub one hand round and round on your stomach.
Stop, then pat the other hand up and down on your head.
Now rub and pat at the same time!

② Circle and "e"

Move one foot round
in a circle like the hands
of a clock.
Stop, then write the letter "**e**"
in the air.
Can you do them together?

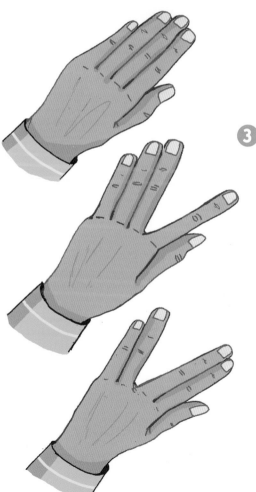

③ Finger fun

Hold out your hand with
your fingers and thumb
together.

Move three fingers away
from two fingers. First one
side, then the other!

Practise and you can get
better!

How do you know what the letter "**e**" looks like?
You remember it! Your memory is part of your brain and
it holds a lot of information. You know how things look,
sound, smell, taste and feel because of your memory.

Which of these foods do you like?

How do you know? You remember!

Now let's exercise your memory. A good memory is very
important. It can help you at school and at home.

Study the twelve things here.
Now close the book!
How many things can you remember?

This brain exercise uses your memory and your nose! Your teacher can help you. Or do it at home with your parents.

You have got
A long scarf

Your teacher has got

8 spoons
A cup of tea without milk
A piece of chocolate
Some soft butter
An orange
Some fish
An apple
A piece of cheese
A banana

You must
Fold the scarf in half. Then close your eyes and tie the scarf round your head, over your eyes.

Your teacher must
Put the food on the spoons. Then hold the spoons in front of your nose one by one.

Can you smell which foods are which?
Now give your friends a turn.

You can exercise your brain
by closing your eyes.

But you can also exercise
your brain by using
your eyes!

1 What do you see in this picture?

Can you see a black vase?
What about two white faces?

2 Which circle in the centre
of the flowers is bigger?

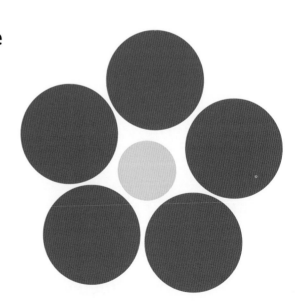

Use your ruler. They are the same size!

3 Look at the centre of the fish for half a minute.
Now look into the bowl. What can you see?
Can you see the fish?

4 Put your fingers together. Now look through your
fingers. Slowly pull your fingers apart. Keep looking
through your fingers. What can you see?

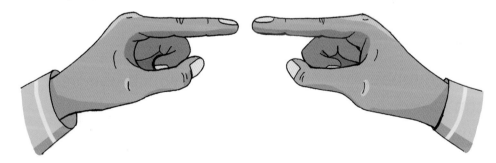

Can you see a floating finger in between?

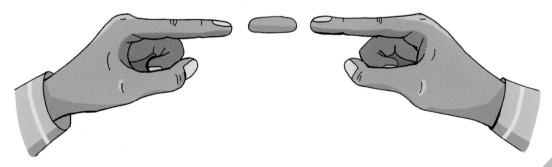

Do you remember all the information which you hear?
You can exercise your brain by listening carefully.
This can help you have a better memory.

Play this game with a friend.

1 Think of a song.
2 Now hum part of the song.
3 Can your friend guess the song?
 Take turns!

You can also exercise your brain by speaking! The best way is by practising tongue twisters.

Here are two excellent examples. Say them out loud and repeat them as fast as you can!

Sue shines shoes.

Seth sells thick socks.

Is your brain tired from so much exercise?
Good!

Eat well, sleep well, and do it all again tomorrow!

Glossary

balancing (n) page 6   not falling over

exercise (n) page 8   an activity to make you stronger

guess (v) page 20   think of an answer

gym (n) cover   a place where you exercise and a sport

information (n) page 14   what you know or can learn

memory (n) page 14   where you keep information in your brain

tongue twisters (n) page 21   things which are difficult to say quickly

Activity page ❶

Before You Read

1 **Look at the cover picture and the title. What is this book about?**

   a Playing sport

   b Sleeping and dreaming

   c Exercising your brain

2 **Read and write True (T) or False (F)?**

   a Your brain is like a very intelligent computer in your head.

   b A bigger brain is more intelligent than a smaller brain.

   c Your nose, eyes and ears can help you exercise your brain.

   d Your brain has different parts.

   e Your brain never gets tired.

Activity page ❷

After You Read

❶ Read and answer Yes (Y) or No (N).

a Can you exercise your memory?

b Can your brain get bigger?

c Does the left half of your brain tell the right side of your body what to do?

❷ Match the words.

1 see   a nose

2 taste   b eyes

3 smell   c ears

4 hear   d tongue

5 feel   e fingers

❸ Copy the picture of the brain. Then label it.

a Balancing

b Seeing

c Smelling and Tasting

d Remembering

e Listening

f Talking

g Moving

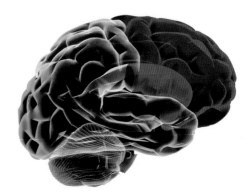